THE 7 SIMPLE TRUTHS OF ACTING FOR THE TEEN ACTOR

OTHER TITLES BY LARRY SILVERBERG

THE 7 SIMPLE TRUTHS OF ACTING FOR THE Teen Actor

Larry Silverberg

YOUNG ACTORS SERIES

Smith and Kraus

Published by Smith and Kraus, Inc.
177 Lyme Road, Hanover, NH 03755
www.smithandkraus.com

First Edition: October 2006
10 9 8 7 6 5 4 3 2 1
Manufactured in the United States of America

Cover and text design by
Julia Hill Gignoux, Freedom Hill Design

Library of Congress Cataloguing-in-Publication Data

Silverberg, L. (Larry)
The 7 simple truths of acting for the teen actor / by Larry Silverberg.
p. cm. — (young actor series)
ISBN 1-57525-462-X
1. Acting. I. Title. II. Title: Seven simple truths of acting for the teen actor.

PN2061.S54 2006
792.02'8—dc22
2006050046

CONTENTS

INTRODUCTION

Man must understand his universe in order to
understand his destiny.

NEIL ARMSTRONG

Why This Book?

If you know that you must act, if your heart is set on it,
this book will give you absolute clarity as to what great
acting is, what it isn't, and how to work toward it. I want
you to be able to recognize and stay very near the people
who can help you grow as a human being and an artist,
and avoid the rest. I am determined to give you the essential information so that you get onto the most useful path
toward fulfilling your dreams. If you are not really sure
yet, if you are just beginning to think that you might like
to become an actor, by the time you finish this book, you
will have a much deeper sense of the true demands of acting, the actor's life, and if any of this is for you.

This past summer, I sat and watched hundreds of
young actors audition for two roles in an Off-Broadway
play I was co-starring in. These parts required actors in
their late teens to early twenties. I was frustrated and sad-
dened to witness 95 percent of these young men and
women acting in the most artificial and deadly manner.
Looking at the résumés of these young people, almost

every one of them had recently completed high school, college, or university actor's training programs. Was I shocked? No, this has been my consistent experience for the past twenty years.

What about the remaining 5 percent of the actors who auditioned? These young people were wonderfully alive, available, and true. They were personally and intimately connected to what they were doing, and they were beautifully simple. Watching them, I forgot all about acting and technique because I was riveted by the life they brought to the very brief moments of the auditions.

I know that you want to be in the 5 percent group. I know that you want to be prepared to either get into a good college to continue your training or to work as an actor when you get out of school. However, much of what you've learned about acting up to this point has not prepared you for professional work. Academic and intellectual theories do not lead to great acting. I've had the benefit of learning from the best teachers and actors in the business. Many instructors have not had this opportunity. In this book, I'm going to share with you a lifetime of real-life discoveries. Whether you're auditioning for college or entering the business, this book will fill you in on what, most likely, your instructors have missed, saving you a lot of time, disappointment, frustration, and money!

Log On and Express Yourself!

Along with buying this book, I am inviting you to join an online forum where you can express your thoughts, concerns, and experiences. As you go through the book, I will ask you questions and give you writing assignments from time to time. Please give these some thought and attention and then log on to my Web site, www.actorscraft.com.

Here you will find the new "Teen Actors Forum" where you can respond to the book and where you can read and learn from the experiences of other teen actors from all around the country.

Lastly . . .

Throughout the book, you will hear me talk about acting in the "theater" and "on the stage." Please know that whenever I talk about acting, I am referring to all acting. This includes performing for film, television, and the stage (as well as CD-ROMs, video games, cell phones, iPods, and any other surprising technology that appears any day now!). Great acting is great acting. The differences in acting for the various mediums are merely technical.

Also, at various points, you will be asked to write down your thoughts in a journal. If you are serious about examining acting, and I hope you are, these will be valuable exercises for you. Get yourself a notebook or journal just for this purpose. It will be a useful tool in your growth process as an actor.

Larry Silverberg

CHAPTER ONE

Truth 1 • Acting Must Relate to Life

R ather than acting in ways guided by how we operate as human beings, most actors manufacture performances out of erroneous notions of what acting is. These performances are always hollow. Our first simple truth of acting states that "acting must relate to life." Let's begin then with an examination of life.

> We cannot climb up a rope that is attached only to our own belt.
>
> WILLIAM ERNEST HOCKING

As this quote shows, life does not work as a solo act. Isn't that true? Unless you're attached to others and to your environment, life is a quick trip downhill. Acting is no different. Much like mountain climbing, to create life onstage requires an act of profound collaboration.

The Story of Life

Here is the story of life broken down into nine principles:

1. Life begins as a true collaboration.
2. Life is a difficult journey.

3. For those who attempt the journey, the odds are against them.

4. Those who attempt the journey must be willing to commit their entire being and to risk everything.

5. Getting closer to accomplishing the goal does not make it easier. The struggle becomes more challenging as the journey continues, requiring greater effort and commitment.

6. Not a moment is casual because the stakes are very high.

7. Complete attention must be placed on what has to be done each step of the way.

8. Finding the path for the journey is not discovered in theories or intellectual studies. The map is only discovered in actually taking the journey.

9. For those who complete the journey, the result is amazing, extraordinary, and unexpected.

Stop a moment. This is important and I don't want you to hurry past this. Please go back and reread the list I just gave you, numbers one through nine. Better yet, take out your journal and write the list down on paper.

Can you see these principles echoed in your life? Because acting must relate to life, these values also resonate throughout the 7 simple truths of acting. These are the most important and fundamental principles of realistic, natural acting. Note these points, study them, and recognize their truth.

Although these nine principles will be thoroughly explored in the following chapters, let's take a closer look at a few of these principles right now.

Collaboration

Men's hearts ought not to be set against one
another, but set with one another, and against
all evil only.

THOMAS CARLYLE

First of all, in every way, acting is a collaborative art. If life onstage is going to occur, the actor must work in true partnership with other people: actors, a director, a stage manager, other crew members, and sometimes directly with the playwright or screenwriter. There is a sense of joy in productions whose creative team members have collaborated with great respect and compassion for each other, let go of the ego in a healthy way, and focused on the creation of a work of art rather than "getting myself a good review." When you have an authentically collaborative environment to work in, it makes the grueling work of acting more than bearable: It becomes thrilling! But true collaboration is not easy. Our society emphasizes competition, furthering the self above all others.

I want you to be the kind of actor that the best creative artists in the world want to work with—and work with again and again. I want people to say what a pleasure it is to have you as part of the creative team; that no matter what the difficulties and challenges are, you are someone who can be counted on every step of the way. And the way to accomplish this is to first become a true collaborator.

I see real collaboration in practice in times of disaster. Out of the terrorist attacks on September 11, 2001, came extraordinary stories of people uniting to help each other. In the documentary *9/11*, filmmaker Gedeon Naudet captured a powerful and simple moment I want to share with you. A short distance from the ongoing tragedy, Naudet captured footage of a large group of people huddled very close together and looking up toward the top of the towers. The group was silent, and all of their faces shared the same look of shock. These people were total strangers of different nationalities and backgrounds, yet watching them in that moment, you could feel how deeply they had become united; in the most profound way, there was no longer any mental, spiritual, or physical separation between them. This diverse group of human beings had truly become one. This was a moment of collaboration.

True collaboration has some particular elements we can identify. There is a common objective, a sense of being accepted, an established state of trust, open communication and participation, and an absence of puffed-up egos. When all of these qualities are present, you have the soil in which true collaboration can grow. However, these qualities must first be recognized and encouraged by the person at the top. The head acting teacher in school or the director of the play must be a real leader. Note that leadership is not the same as dictatorship. A dictator, or autocrat, encourages competitiveness and seeks to control, which sabotages and paralyzes the creative gifts of every member of the group.

The Monarchy School of Acting

When you are in a class or a play, ask yourself these questions: Do you feel really accepted? Do you experience a sense of trust in the group? Do you feel that you are as important to the group as everyone else in the room? Do you feel safe to express your honest feelings? Are you made to believe that what you have to say is as welcomed, listened to, and really heard by the teacher/director and the other students/actors? Do you feel like an equal participant of the group? When you are working, do you have the real interest and attention of the teacher/director and the other actors? In short, do you feel like your acting teacher or director invests energy and time into establishing the qualities of true collaboration in your classes and in the play rehearsals?

If not, you may be entered in what I like to call the monarchy school of acting. In this school, the teacher/director is king and wishes to be praised and honored above all else. Below the king comes the prince and the princess, the school stars who get the lead roles year after year, and receive all of the king's attention and affection. Next in line are the loyal servants to the king who work very hard to gain recognition and respect for their efforts, though their efforts are often in vain.

This unhealthy environment springs from the true intention of the person in charge. These programs breed jealousy, resentment, insecurity, sadness, contempt, anger, hostility, self-consciousness, hurt, and hopelessness. The acting that results from this style of acting program is usually very slick and completely meaningless. Because of the slickness, the school may even win itself some awards, but the students have learned nothing of value, and many people have been damaged and discouraged along the way.

How do you perform and thrive under these circumstances? The truth is, you can't. If you discover that you are in the monarchy school of acting, remove yourself from this unhealthy environment. This teacher acts like the king because of one reason: He is actually terrified because he does not really know how to help you. He knows that if he is found out, he may lose his job.

And what if you are lucky enough to have a

wonderful acting teacher who recognizes the rigorous demands of true acting? My strong suggestion is to pour your heart and soul into it. Always be on time, and always be prepared to work. In fact, be more than prepared than you think is necessary. Do more work than is asked of you. Find ways to encourage other students; when they take a risk in class, say how impressed you are with their courage. Ask your teacher if there is anything you can do to assist her or him. Before class begins, make sure the room is clean and ready to work in. When class ends, clean the space so it is ready for whoever comes there next. Enlist others in the group to help you. Make this your home. Devote yourself to it as if it were a sacred place, because it is.

What has your own experience been? Have you personally experienced the monarchy school of acting or are you one of the fortunate young actors who have a truly collaborative environment in your classes and plays? Log on to www.actorscraft.com, go to the Teen Actors section, and express yourself!

The Journey Is Difficult

Character cannot be developed in ease and quiet. Only through experience of trial and suffering can the soul be strengthened, ambition inspired, and success achieved.

HELEN KELLER

I am not afraid of storms for I am learning how to sail my ship.

LOUISA MAY ALCOTT

If you really look around, you will see that all of nature shares in a basic understanding—that life itself requires hard work and effort. When my daughter was a baby learning to walk, she went through all of the typical phases. At about four months old, I would hold her upright and she'd bounce up and down on her feet; she perfected rolling over, crawling, and sitting, all the while developing her leg muscles for the ultimate aim of getting up and walking like the rest of us. At about seven-and-a-half months, she began pulling herself up to standing position by holding onto the furniture. After a few weeks of practicing this move, she would get around the room by holding onto various pieces of furniture. Finally, at nine months old, she took her first steps. These were months of very rigorous and consistent work on her part and, of course, there were many falls and bruises—but when she fell, she never sat around calling herself a bad person and she never gave up, she simply tried again. She made attempt after attempt, with no complaints, until she reached her goal.

Renowned author and children's advocate Dr. Benjamin Spock said that children love learning not because it is easy but because it is hard. Although most adults try to make things easier on themselves, children purposely invent ways to make their activities more difficult; they have an inborn enjoyment in being challenged. Look at skateboarders who are not satisfied riding on flat pavement, they need the intense difficulty of half-pipes and grind ledges. Since learning about camping, my son would never light a campfire with a match when he could utilize the primitive method of "rubbing sticks." Making an activity harder places greater demands on the person doing it and calls for a greater willingness to take a risk—

risking that it won't be accomplished and risking looking foolish.

This is an important point, so take note. When you have to do something that is meaningful to you, achievement requires great effort and engagement in the task. The more effort and engagement you give the task, the greater the payoff when it is accomplished. Ralph Waldo Emerson wisely said,

> Do not be too timid and squeamish about your actions. All life is an experiment. The more experiments you make the better. What if they are a little coarse, and you may get your coat soiled or torn? What if you do fail, and get fairly rolled in the dirt once or twice. Up again, you shall never be so afraid of a tumble.

Here's another example of this point from the natural world. Because light is the major source of energy for plants, they will grow toward the light to enhance their ability to gather it. Here is an enlightening experiment for you to try. Make a maze of dividers inside a cardboard box. Cut a hole at one end of the box for light to enter, place a bean plant at the other end and make a little trap door to water it. Then, except for the little light hole, cover the whole thing with black paper. After a few days, you will find that the bean plant will actually wind its way around the dividers as it fights its way to the light. Eventually, with no hard feelings toward you for giving it a hard time, the bean plant will grow all the way out of the hole.

In the documentary film, *March of the Penguins*, we witness the astonishing physical struggle emperor penguins must endure for the welfare of their families. In the thousands, the penguins leave the water and head off on snow-covered ice for a trip to the breeding ground, which takes many days. Once there, and without the help of Internet dating services, the penguins search for a partner, pair off, and mate. By the time the females lay the eggs, they have lost up to a third of their weight. Soon, with great care, the males take the eggs so that the females can make the long trek back to the water for food. Now, without having eaten in two months, the males will attempt to keep the eggs warm (by balancing the eggs on top of their feet!) in winds over 120 miles per hour and temperatures plunging to fifty degrees below zero. In the most extraordinary example of collaboration, the males huddle together for nearly a month while the females are away, taking turns bringing their eggs to the middle of the huge circle where the icy wind is mildest. Before the mother penguins return, the eggs hatch. The chicks can now survive for only a few days, living on a very small secretion fed to them by the males. When the females return, they regurgitate food to feed the youngsters who have survived. The male, who has lost about thirty pounds, now takes his turn to go back to the sea for nourishment. No one can doubt the difficulty of this journey, but this does not discourage or defeat the penguins' resolve to succeed.

If we examine the nature of all sports, we can see clearly that the games are purposely challenging. It seems silly to even imagine a sport being easy to do. Can you imagine playing on a professional basketball league where the hoop was four feet off of the ground rather then ten? What about a baseball league where the person at bat was called out after forty strikes rather than three or where the pitcher's mound was five feet from home plate rather then fifty-nine feet? What if cross-country running was won by the person who took the *most* time?

Would it be very interesting to either the person in the race or to the person watching it?

The truth is, we know that anything of value in this life is difficult. If you play a musical instrument, you know the huge challenges involved; mastering any instrument requires hours of daily practice. If guitar is your passion, you know how painful it was at first to press the strings down hard enough to get a clear sounding note. But over time, the ends of your fingers got tough and calloused and you began to make beautiful sounds. If you study ballet, you expect your feet to hurt, and you know it will take years of consistent work to master a triple pirouette. And so both the guitarist and the dancer know that there is no way around the pain, you simply have to work through it. Wynton Marsalis, winner of the Pulitzer Prize for Music said,

> I practiced every day. I went about seven years without missing a day of practice. I had a very strict schedule that I would follow, and I would not go to sleep until I had practiced all the stuff I had to practice.

Olympic skater Scott Hamilton said it this way,

> You've got to fall down a lot. You've got to make a lot of mistakes. And you've got to fight for your place in the world, whatever it is. And you've got to take a lot of knocks, and you've got to spill some blood in order to get there. And that's part of the process.

Why should acting be any different? Most actors try to make acting comfortable, they don't want to sweat, and they don't want to struggle. It's easier to make a face here and do an inflection there because the truth is, it is much easier to pretend, to fake, and to lie than it is to work authentically. Playwright David Mamet said that the difference between the actor who fakes his way through a performance and the actor who brings his soul to the stage is like the difference between a fluorescent light and a wood-burning fire.

So I ask you, which would you rather resemble, a fluorescent light or a wood-burning fire? Please take a moment and write about this in your journal. What does it mean to be like a wood-burning fire rather than a fluorescent light? What does it mean to work really hard, to work "through the pain"? What has your experience been so far in your training regarding these values? Have you brought yourself to the work fully? If you would like to share your thoughts, please log on to www.actorscraft.com, go to the Teen Actors section, and express yourself!

Why Choose Acting?

So, why would anyone choose to tackle this demanding art form? This is an art in which the artist has no strings on an instrument, no brush, no paints, and no canvas to help him or her create. Why would anyone choose to stand in front of a room filled with strangers and, in the most intimate way, make art using only his or her own voice, body, heart, mind, and guts?

The answer is that 95 percent of actors don't choose acting to strive toward making art; they choose acting because, thanks to the great actors, it looks easy. Isn't that true of the masters in any field? When I watch my video of Isaac Stern playing the violin, I almost believe that with a few lessons I could do it, too! The other big reason many people choose acting is the lure of nice clothes, big houses, sex, and fame. You know, the lottery commercials also make it look easy, but just like the ninety-nine out of a hundred ticket holders who lose their money, the great majority of people who choose acting as an easy route to fame will soon drop by the wayside.

Remember from the introduction that 5 percent of great actors who caught my attention and admiration? They know that to be a true actor there is a cost. These are the people who welcome the rigorous and deeply personal work involved in honing one's craft. These are the rare human beings who embrace the grueling demands of preparing for auditions and who rise above the exhaustion of bringing oneself fully to every moment of an intense rehearsal schedule and eight performances a week. These are the courageous artists who are willing and able to take the risk of entering the unknown both in the small community of the rehearsal hall and the larger community of an audience. Why is it that these people have chosen to act? I say that, in fact, they have not chosen to act; like falling in love, acting has chosen them—and there is no escape.

Now, this is a dangerous notion to bring into our discussion because most people use the concept of fate as an excuse not to make any real effort. My own belief is that you and I are here on this planet to do something very important, to make a difference and to fight for something. I believe that whatever the thing is that we have come here to do, it was planted in us by the time we were born. I also believe that the way we discover our destiny is through hard work, without any expectation for what the results may be. Often, where we end up is not where we thought we were going.

This is what I know about fate: If we commit to one thing and bring ourselves to it completely, doors open up that we could not even have imagined before. The point I am making here is that I do not want you to worry about the end result. Will you become an actor? Are you "talented" enough? If you work hard, you will develop your gifts and if you don't work hard, you won't. Please try not to worry about your destiny right now. Turn your full attention to what is in front of you here and now. And listen. Listen carefully to what is happening all around you. Listen quietly to what is happening deep inside you. Keep listening . . .

CHAPTER TWO

Truth 2 • You Are the Character

Every artist dips his brush into his own soul, and
paints his own nature into his pictures.
                                    HENRY WARD BEECHER

It's really very simple. Now and for the rest of your life, no matter what part you play, the character is always you. From my point of view, that's the good news! Most actors do not welcome this essential aspect of great acting, which is why their performances are nothing more than imitations of what they have seen before. As a result, they always act the cliché of the given circumstances.

> *Cliché: something that has lost its original effectiveness or power from overuse*

> *Given Circumstances: the physical and emotional conditions the character is living in*

How do we avoid the cliché in our acting? That's a very good question. I hope that you are truly interested in the answer because it is not easy. You must become rigorously honest with yourself. To better understand how you "become" a character, it is imperative to first grapple with your own character and come to grips with the role you play in your own life.

Who Are You Really?

Let's begin with some basic psychological concepts. In infancy, everyone is fully expressive. It is completely natural for us to cry without worrying about what other people think of us. It is easy to scream without the fear that we are being too loud. It is effortless to laugh in the most exuberant way without worrying that people may think us idiotic. As infants, we don't censor our responses because we are not concerned with looking good; the possibility of appearing foolish never crosses our minds. For the first few years of our life, we remain completely honest about how we feel toward the people and the world around us.

We are also born with a powerful desire to survive. And as we grow, survival means figuring out what wins the approval of our parents, what behavior helps us navigate the complex currents of life at school, and what kind of person we should be to get our friends to like us. From our hair and clothes to the way we walk and talk, we become very concerned about looking good and not looking foolish. We whittle down our self-expression to such a degree that our natural self becomes barely visible. The outcome of this process is the role we decide to play in our life. As time goes by, although not at a conscious level, we identify with the role we mold to such a degree that it becomes who we believe ourselves to wholly be.

Here's an example from my life. Back in high school, I remember being shocked to hear someone describing me as "that quiet and intense guy." I remember going home and giving it a lot of thought. I realized that night, that the person who described me was right; even though I didn't consciously think of myself as quiet and intense, that is exactly how I appeared to the world around me. I had become the character called "Larry, the quiet and intense guy." Looking back, I know that a big part of my decision to play that role was my acute self-consciousness from being a very fat child. But was "quiet and intense" all that I was? No, of course not, I was actually all kinds of things—silly, loud, contemplative, energetic, serious, goofy, etc.—but how could I possibly take the risk and let everyone see these parts of me? It was much safer to be quiet and intense.

Why do you think I felt safer playing the part of the quiet and intense guy? It had to do with control. Much of our effort to play our chosen role is aimed at controlling others' thoughts and behaviors toward us. But the truth is, it's a futile effort. Is it really possible to control what other people think about us? Is it possible to control how other people feel? No, of course not. Yet we put so much energy into the act. It's like trying to make someone fall in love with you; it can't be done!

Another thing to take note of is that the role we develop and play in public is often different than the role we play at home with the people closest to us. With our family, we usually allow ourselves to express more of who we are. So we have a self we show in public situations, another self we show to our families, and then we have a very private self that we only reveal to ourselves. This last self, the private self, is the part of us we keep hidden from the world, the part that holds our most personal thoughts and feelings.

I want you to give this some thought. If someone you don't know too well at school described you to someone else, what do you think he or she would say? Can you define the role you play when you are out in public? Can you see a difference between the "you" at school and the "you" at home with your family? How do these roles relate to your private self, the "you" of your most personal thoughts and feelings? Take some time to write about this in your journal.

Remember, as an infant, we were completely ourselves; we had no role to play, and we had no desire to control anyone or anything. For the first few years we were spontaneous, authentic human beings. Isn't that what we must aim for in our acting? Yes, it is. This is why most adults love being with babies and very young children. Infants remind adults of who they once were— open, receptive, simple, and fully alive! Great actors do the same, they remind the people in the audience how fully alive they once were and that being fully alive is still possible.

I want to be very clear that I am not saying that role-playing in life is a bad thing; it is not bad or wrong, however, it is limiting. As an actor, if we can't shed these layers of control mechanisms and self-protectiveness, our acting will be extremely restricted. It's like painting: The painter wants to begin with a clean canvas. If he starts out with a canvas that has paint all over it, the effort to paint his own, original work of art will be much more difficult.

Let's go back to the statement "the character is always you . . . and that's the good news!" Let's break it down into two sections.

The Character Is Always You

Most actors think that by doing a limp or talking with a lisp or wearing cool sunglasses, they've created a character. Of course, this is very far from the truth. These kinds of choices may ultimately be good or bad for the character you are playing, but on their own, they do not define character. They are only external clues and do not involve the person within.

Look at it this way: Whose heart is racing and whose underarms are sweaty before your big entrance in Act One? Whose voice is saying your lines? Whose body is wearing your itchy costume? That person is *you*. In the journey toward character, you must begin simply with yourself. If you don't, you will end up with an empty shell that does not resemble a live, human being. "But," you might say, "I am nothing like the character I have to play." Ah-ha! Now you're on to it. Here's part two:

That's the Good News!

As a human being, you have inherited every experience known to human beings throughout time. It's all inside you already; it's in your DNA! That's the good news. You do not need to look outside yourself to play a character because he or she is already a part of you. So rather than putting on a mask to try and become a character, I want you to think of peeling away masks layer by layer to reveal the character within. Isn't that an exciting way to look at the work you have to do?

I hope that you will grow to truly love this aspect of your job as an actor. It is through the process of digging and searching inside yourself that you will find the most intimate connections you have with the character. In this way, there is no need to hide behind a smoke screen. Just like the Wizard who hid behind his curtain, afraid Dorothy and her buddies would see what a phony he actually was, most actors hide behind their limps and lisps, trying hard not to be discovered for the impostors they actually are.

Because this is a big deal, here again is the simple equation to remember:

Putting on masks to become a character = Bad acting
Peeling away masks to reveal the character = Good acting

Since we are on this topic, I need to clarify a couple of acting concepts for you. Have you heard of acting from the "inside-out" and acting from the "outside-in"? Acting from the inside-out is how most people would describe modern American acting technique. It refers to the process of using one's own inner life to bring psychological and emotional reality to the stage. This is what most people think of when they talk about Method acting. (I will talk more about Method acting in chapter 5.)

Acting from the outside-in is when an actor begins with a purely physical trait to approach playing a part. The crucial thing in this approach is that the actor who begins with an outside physical trait must ultimately unearth the psychological and emotional truth just as in the inside-out approach. For instance, if you walk with a severe limp, this will have a deep impact on your attitude toward life and the world all around you. Some very clear examples of physical conditions having a profound influence on the characters' psychological and emotional life are Laura in *The Glass Menagerie*, the Hunchback in *The Hunchback of Notre Dame*, and John Merrick in *The*

Elephant Man. Their physical conditions made them retreat from society, affecting their self-esteem and numerous other inner traits. See how that works?

Limps and lisps are called physical impediments. Many characters have some sort of physical impediment that you will have to perform behaviorally. These physical impediments are a technical challenge and must be worked on meticulously until they occur naturally and habitually, without conscious thought. As you work with the physical condition, you must process how it affects you internally and discover how it shapes your point of view toward the world.

Point of View

And there they are, the three words that I have been working toward throughout this chapter—point of view. So here now are our working definitions of character and point of view:

> *character: a specific point of view*

> *point of view: a particular way of thinking about or approaching a subject, as shaped by a person's own experience, mindset, and history*

For us actors, the words *point of view* are huge. They are the source of what makes each of us unique in this world, and they are the key to inhabiting the character in the play. So "character" is not the physical condition of a person, how a person is treated by his or her parents growing up, the kind of house he or she lives in, or the kind of shoes he or she wears—it is how *all* of these things shape a person's insides, which then results in how the person responds to the people and events in his or her life. And just as you and I have a right to our own point of view, the character has a right to his or hers. So, when we read a script in preparation for playing one of the roles, it is our job to come to grips with the character's point of view toward the other characters in the play, toward the circumstances he or she is involved in, and toward the world in which he or she lives.

By now, I'm sure you see that my strong belief is that everything we do as an actor must relate to our lives and how we behave in the world. If getting onto intimate terms with our character's point of view is our job, it is important that we first get onto intimate terms with our own point of view. To do this, I am going to give you two writing exercises. Both will involve free-association writing. Free-association writing means that you do not stop to think about what to write. You simply write down whatever pops into your mind without judgment. So in the following exercises, when you are ready, I want you to launch yourself into writing. Write very fast, and do not stop writing until you have filled one page.

The Joyous Object

Go to your room and pick out an object that when you look at it, hold it, or think about it, it gives you a deep sense of joy and happiness; it just makes you feel good inside. (For example, the object can be a stuffed animal, a photograph, a poem, or lyrics to a favorite song.) Once you have the object, open your journal to a blank page. Begin writing a free association about this object and everything it means to you. Again, write fast and do not stop. Let the words pour out of you, through the pen, and onto the paper until you have filled the entire page.

The Enraging Article

Read the newspaper or look online at a news Web site and choose an article that makes you very angry, so angry you want to scream. Once you have found the article, open your journal to a new blank page. Tape the article onto the back of the opposite page and read the article again. Then, write a free association on the blank page. Write everything you have to say about this article and why it makes you so mad. Write very fast and do not stop until you have filled the entire page.

By doing these two writing assignments, you have begun the process of exploring your own point of view. This is a wonderful process for you to start now since you are at a time in life when you are independently forming many strong beliefs about life. Down the road, the payoff in your acting will be huge.

CHAPTER THREE

Truth 3 • The Words Are the Tip of the Iceberg

Do not the most moving moments of our lives
find us all without words?

MARCEL MARCEAU

You were born without verbal language. As an infant, words had no meaning to you. When your mother whispered in your ear how much she loved you, it wasn't really the words that soothed you; it was the meaning behind them. If you were in the room while your parents were arguing, you may not have understood what they said, but the emotional implications behind the words upset you. The point I am making here is that when you were a baby, even though you didn't know what the words meant, you understood the meaning behind the words—not in your head—but more importantly, deep down inside where you live!

This essential aspect of communication is still true for you today. Have you ever had the experience where you knew what someone meant even when the words weren't quite right? Or have you been with someone who was so emotional they could not utter a word, yet you knew exactly what they were trying to say?

Communicating

The truth is, words are imperfect, so to get our message across, body language is key. Body language is made up of our physical gestures, facial expressions, our posture and movements, and the tone, volume, and inflection of our voice. Scientific research has shown that nonverbal cues account for over 90 percent of our overall communication. Research also proves that body language is used especially to express what is hardest to put into words—our feelings. And almost all of the time, our body language is happening without any conscious intention on our part. Let me highlight this vital point: *Body language happens without any conscious intention on our part.*

This is a critical fact to take note of, but most actors totally ignore it. Most actors *think* up clever gestures to show how they *think* the character would act in order to express what they *think* the character means. You may have noticed that I just used the word *think* three times. That's because these actors are in their heads; they approach playing the role intellectually. And because this is not a natural way of working, their performances are fake.

Why are we talking about body language anyway? The author gives us real language, right? We just need to say the words the playwright wrote. But doesn't this lead us down the same road; don't we end up *thinking* about how to say the text? We need to find the feelings and motivations behind physical and spoken language.

Truth 3 is "the words are the tip of the iceberg." Ninety percent of an iceberg is underwater and cannot be seen; the iceberg is mostly a massive, unseen formation. The underwater base of the iceberg is like our nonverbal communication. It's the foundation for our feelings, attitudes, wants and desires. The tip of the iceberg, the 10 percent that's clearly visible, is like the words we actually speak. As the great theater director Peter Brook said, words are always the last thing to occur. They're built upon the deep need for expression. The wants and desires always come before the words. So you see, the words—like the tip of the iceberg—are the most superficial layer, which emerges from a massive, unseen desire to communicate.

Your job as an actor has much more to do with the unseen formation that makes the words necessary than with the words themselves. The words, my friends, are the easy part! When you have a true need to speak the character's words, your body language and the actual text come to life without any effort on your part. Isn't this fantastic? When you have a personal connection to your character's wants and desires, your words will be alive and the audience will witness a bona fide human being onstage rather than an actor showing off his or her slick technique. Isn't this why people pay (sometimes over a hundred dollars) to go to the theater? To witness real human beings in the midst of extreme circumstances, fighting against all odds?

Because you must make deep, personal contact with the people, places, and things that have great meaning to the character, it is useful to first understand what has great meaning to you. Please take out your journal. Write again in the form of a free association: very fast and without pausing to think about what to say. Keep that pen moving!

Write about a moment or an event that had a major contribution on who you are today. Get writing!

Write about the person you are closest to in the entire world. Describe both the person and why you feel so close with her or him. Write now!

The Place of Really Knowing

If you did the assignment, I have a question for you. Where would you say all the words you wrote down came from? I describe it this way: The words came from a place of *really knowing*. As you wrote about the special moment in your life and about the person you are closest with in the entire world, you wrote about things you truly know. I do not mean you "know" as some sort of concept, but I mean you "know" deep down inside! And, if you were talking about these things with me in person, all of your behavior—both verbal and nonverbal—would be filled with life because you would be speaking from a place of truth. The same is true of every character in every well-written play, they are speaking from a place of really knowing; they know what they are talking about because their words originated in the heart, mind, and guts of the playwright.

The challenge is, though the playwright knows the character inside and out, you don't! To claim your right to speak those words, you have to do your homework. This is one of our huge challenges as actors. You have to know what your character is talking about as strongly and deeply as you know the important moment in your life and the person you are closest to in the entire world. This is a process called "personalization" or "making the words your own." This process takes place during your rehearsals. (To try and teach you how to personalize the character's words would take up an entire book, which is why I wrote one. My book *The Sanford Meisner Approach, Workbook Four: Playing the Part* will give you very specific instructions on how to personalize the text.)

Why is it so important to personalize the words? Why is it essential that you know deep down what you are talking about when you speak the character's words? Why can't you simply memorize your lines and deliver them as loud and clear as you can?

Don't pull back now and allow the dark side to suck you in! Remember, you are here to strive toward being in that 5 percent group of actors; the rare group of actors who live vibrantly, honestly, and passionately onstage and who make a true difference in the lives of the people who come to the theater. David Mamet said that people still go to the theater "to be reminded that authentic communication between two human beings is still possible."

Receiving

Now let's flip the coin. We just talked about how we communicate to others. Now let's look at how we receive what is being communicated to us. Certainly we use all of our senses:

1. We *hear* what she says to us.

2. We *see* her body language.

3. We *feel* her hold our hand.

4. We *smell* her perfume.

5. We *taste* the kiss on her lips.

But these physical senses are not the whole story. In addition to the use of our physical senses, there is a more mysterious sixth sense we use and it is called intuition.

intuition: knowing something subconsciously, without actual evidence

Intuition is just as accurate and real as any of our physical senses. Regardless of whether we are conscious of it or whether we choose to trust, ignore, or deny it, our intuitive powers are in operation all of the time. I would say that a big portion of how we perceive what is really happening with another person is intuitive.

The Crucial Connection

On one side we have a person communicating (90 percent of which is through body language and without conscious intention). On the other side we have a person receiving the communication (which is largely intuitive and without conscious effort on their part). When these two people are really open and available to each other, there is what I call an "invisible thread" that connects them. This is the crucial connection.

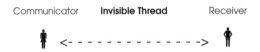

Communicator   **Invisible Thread**   Receiver

Now, why is all of this so important? Well, first of all, this invisible thread is exactly what exists between you and your partners onstage when you are working well. It also creates the connection, when you are working authentically, that exists between you and the audience. Without this thread, you are working on your own without any connection to the world around you. This is a dangerous place to be in; it's like driving down the highway at seventy miles an hour while looking in your vanity mirror—you will most likely get into a horrendous accident. And this is exactly what most actors are doing onstage, they are busy watching themselves, either criticizing their own performance as they perform or they are congratulating themselves for how well it's going. If you work with this kind of actor, you may as well be doing a solo act. This ego-driven actor will end up making both you and the audience bored, repulsed, and depressed.

Here's a short story from my own experience. In acting school, my classmates and I had become true family to each other. In our training with the great acting teacher of our time, Sanford Meisner, we worked in an environment of trust, honesty, and real collaboration—it was the best of all worlds. A few weeks after graduating, I was cast in a co-starring part in a big Off-Broadway production. Of course, I was very excited to get my first real acting job. However, late in rehearsals, a pretty well-known actor left the production. I thought this was strange. Here we were, soon to open our play in a beautiful theater right off of Broadway in Times Square, and this guy was quitting. It wasn't until we opened the play and were in performances for a few weeks that the lightbulb lit up and I finally understood why this actor had left the production.

My co-star was completely unavailable to me; it was like acting in a vacuum. In every scene, his eyes were glazed over and I could tell he was much more concerned about what the audience was thinking of his performance than anything that might be going on with me. That stage became the loneliest place in the world. Although this was a painful experience for me, I learned an important lesson. Since then, I have not allowed myself to be in a position where I have to work with such a selfish and self-absorbed actor.

Let's review. We established today that the words you speak only tell part of the story. What is not said is as important or even more important than what is spoken. We also determined that, just as in life itself, the underlying wants and desires of the character drive the words to the surface. If you get on intimate terms with the character's very human needs, you will effortlessly be a living, breathing human being when you act. When you boil it all down, your job as an actor is to live onstage. I do not mean to pretend to live, which is what most actors do, but to actually live, to get to that place of "really knowing."

We also talked about how people receive communication. In addition to all of the physical senses, we also use our intuition. If you are working well, the audience is connecting to you both on an intellectual level (they see you and hear your words, etc.) and on an intuitive level (they understand the more intimate feelings beneath the words). In short, they are experiencing a life. Whose life? Your life! You are the character—remember?

CHAPTER FOUR

Truth 4 • Your Acting Is Alive or It Is Dead

Men are born soft and supple; dead, they are stiff and hard. Plants are born tender and pliant; dead, they are brittle and dry. The hard and stiff will be broken. The soft and supple will prevail.

Nothing in the world is as soft and yielding as water. Yet for dissolving the hard and inflexible, nothing can surpass it. The soft overcomes the hard; the gentle overcomes the rigid. Everyone knows this is true, but few can put it into practice.

TAO TE CHING

I begin with two wonderful quotes from *Tao Te Ching* because they illuminate the differences between life and death in a living thing. Of course, what we desire is to be more alive in our acting but because of bad training, most actors work in a deadly manner; they are stiff, inflexible, and rigid.

So the question is, how do you become soft and yielding as water yet, just like water, strong enough to wear down stone when necessary? How do you work in ways that will always lead to aliveness? There are some key factors. Let's jump in.

Listen with the Ear of Your Heart

Many acting teachers talk about "listening" as a technical skill. These teachers also preach the importance of "eye contact" as if it was the main indication that actors were really "in touch" with each other. What all of this mechanical garbage produces in the acting student is a lot of ineffective effort and false behavior. I can't tell you how many bulging eyes I have seen in actors trying to stay "in contact" with their acting partners onstage. It's pathetic and, believe me, it is the teacher's fault for encouraging such nonsense!

The truth is that both listening and eye contact happen naturally and effortlessly when you are working in the right way, and the right way is called being *truly available*. When you are truly available to your partners onstage, you don't have to think about your ears and your eyes; they perform their functions quite genuinely and with no effort at all. Listening and looking are no longer technical feats because you are available at a deeper level. I call it listening with the ear of one's heart. This suggests that rather than just being conscious of the other actors onstage in your head, you are now available to these human beings down where you live!

Imagine trying to put fresh cut flowers into a vase that is tightly sealed with many layers of clear wrap. Not seeing the clear wrap, you go to put the flowers into the vase, but they are rejected because the vase is closed up. To get the flowers into the vase you would have to rip and tear the clear wrap away. Or you might use the stems of the flowers in a violent jab and puncture the clear wrap to gain entrance. Of course, if the clear wrap were not there, putting the flowers into the vase would be effortless because the vase would be ready to accept them just as it was created to do. My friend, you and I are the vase and as actors, it is our job to "unwrap" ourselves, so that we become what we were designed to be—completely open and receptive!

When you are listening with the ear of your heart, people are drawn to you and they open to you in beautiful and unexpected ways. Just today, on line at the local supermarket, I wheeled my cart toward the checkout lanes and I was greeted by a cashier, a middle-aged woman with a big smile. I smiled back and asked her how she was doing. She looked into my eyes and then leaned over suddenly, her elbows resting on the counter, her eyes looking down at her clasped hands. She couldn't talk for a few moments. Finally, she raised her head, holding back tears, and said, "I don't know." She looked at me, shook her head a little, and repeated, "I don't know." Then we talked, and I learned that the cashier, Lisa, still lives with her mom. Although she always thought she would have lots of children, it didn't turn out that way. Though she tried to smile the whole time, I felt her sadness and her loneliness. As I took my bags to leave, Lisa came out from behind her register and gave me a big hug. It was a powerful reminder of how simply being available to another human being can produce this kind of surprising event. I consider it a little miracle.

And so it is onstage. When you are listening with the ear of your heart, the other actors are drawn to you because they have the wonderful experience of how *present* you are. The audience is also drawn to your *presence* and though they can't express it in words, they fall in love with you from their seats in the house.

Be in the Present

Here it is, our next key factor in aliveness: presence or being in the present.

Let's go to the definition in my Microsoft Word dictionary:

> *presence: the quality of certain performers that enables them to achieve a rapport with and hold the attention of their audiences*

To be very clear, when I talk about presence, I am not talking about anything to do with personality or charisma; I am talking about the ability to live fully in this moment right now. As opposed to where we have our attention most of the time—either on what's coming up in the future or what has happened in the past—life is really only available to us in this moment right now. Acting is the art of right now. Say these words:

> *Right now, right now, right now, right now, right now, right now, right now.*

As soon as you say "now," you are led to the next "right now" in order to be truly in the present. Here's a little assignment for you. The next time you are doing any activity—washing the dishes, eating breakfast, folding your clothes—try to take note of what thoughts are running through your head. Are they about something that has happened earlier in the day or yesterday or last week? Are they about something you are planning to do that night or tomorrow or next week? See if you can let go of all of those thoughts and give your full, undivided attention to the thing you are doing in the present moment. All

I am asking you to do is to notice. Noticing is the first step toward strengthening your ability to stay in the present rather then in the past or the future.

As infants, we always had our attention on what was happening in the present moment. Of course animals live their entire lives in this manner. Is a dog ever late? This is why you may have heard it said that if you work onstage with a young child or an animal, the audience's attention will always be on the child or the animal and not on you.

Imagine a cat onstage playing with a ball of yarn. As the cat plays, do you think he is having thought's like, "Hey, I am really wowing the audience with my great athletic abilities!" or, "Damn, I did this yarn scene much better last night!" or, "Man, if they like this yarn bit, wait until they see my next scene where I wrestle with the toy mouse!" Of course the cat isn't thinking these things, only bad actors have these kinds of thoughts while they are performing. The child's and the cat's ability to be fully immersed in the present moment is one of the main ingredients that captivates the audience and pulls in their attention.

Isn't it interesting that even the definition we found in the dictionary recognizes that only "certain performers" have the quality of presence that "holds the attention" of the people in the audience. This is absolutely true. Ninety-five percent of actors are not really present to anything because they are busy in their heads going over how they did in the scene before, watching themselves in the middle of the current scene, and preparing for the "big moment" they will have in the scene coming next. These actors are not really present to anything that is actually happening. I want you to hear this loud and clear, it is that important! These actors are not really present to anything that is actually happening.

The Reality of Doing

Once you are fully living in the present, it allows the blossoming of our next key factor, which will lead to acting that is alive rather than dead. My great teacher, Sanford Meisner, called it the Reality of Doing.

This means that when you do something onstage, you don't pretend to do it and you don't fake doing it, you *really do it*. What exactly does this mean? Sandy (as we called him) once told us a story, which was a great example of the reality of doing. A previous student came to him with a problem he was having with a moment in a play. The student had to ask the female character to marry him. When this moment happened, the director wanted this man to break down and cry. The actor told Sandy that he was having a hard time with this moment. Sandy told the actor "If you want to handle that acting challenge, when you ask the girl to marry you, *really ask her to marry you.*"

Sounds simple right? Sandy always helped his students simplify their acting by finding the most human solutions. Note that Sandy did not tell this actor to think of a time his dog died so that he could cry, and he did not tell the actor to pretend to cry. He told the actor to really do what he was doing—to really ask the girl to marry him. In this way, the actor would have to put his own life into those four precious words, "Will you marry me?"

What I want you to understand here is that it is not an actor's job to illustrate the words so that the audience will understand the story. Do you know what I mean by illustrate? Let's say in scene two of the play, the character Cindy is very sad because she just found out that she got a failing grade in math class. So, the actress playing the role of Cindy makes a sad expression with her face and sad sounds with her voice to make it *look* like she is sad. This is called "illustrating the words" or "indication," and it is nothing more than a lie. And no matter how slick the actor is, the audience knows deep down that they are being lied to.

I want you to know that the only thing that truly communicates to the audience and hits them where they live is your actual experience in the moment. So, when I tell you that you must really *do* onstage, I am saying that when you must be enraged in a moment of the play, you must actually *be* enraged, or when you must be filled with joy in a moment of the play, you must actually *be* filled with joy! Is this making sense to you? I hope you see this as a much more exciting and invigorating way of working. Of course, it places greater demands on you in many ways, but the payoff in terms of aliveness is huge! Now, what we have is a living, breathing human being onstage, actually experiencing the things he or she is going through. We also have an audience that feels like they are witnessing something so real that they forget they are watching actors in a play.

No Moment Is Casual

Now, just like the actor who had to ask the girl to marry him, plays and screenplays are made up of characters that are involved in doing things that have great meaning to them. If you remember back in chapter 1, the sixth in our list of nine principles stated: "Not a moment is casual because the stakes are very high."

It is vital that you come to grips with the fact that in a play not one single moment is casual. In our lives too there is much at stake. It is usually only in the midst of very extreme circumstances that we are reawakened to this fact. Here are a few examples. Imagine the person you love most in the world was trapped in a burning car. Where would all of your attention be? Yes, it would be on getting the person out of the car. And if you were sewing a rip in a dress you were going to wear on your first big date, where would your attention be? Yes, your attention would be on sewing the dress perfectly. If your mom had been feeling depressed, and you were decorating a cake for her birthday to show her how special she was to you, where would all of your attention be? Yes, it would be on making a beautiful cake for your mom. In all of these examples, you would really *do* the things you had to do. Because you were actually doing them and because you were giving them your full attention due to their importance to you, they would demand the attention of anyone who was observing you. You see, when you really do something and when the thing you are doing has great meaning to you, the doing of it brings you to life; you become incredibly interesting to watch.

When you start to really *do* things onstage, there will be a revolution in your work as an actor! I want to impress upon you the urgency with which you must tackle this ingredient in your acting. This alone will raise your work above 95 percent of actors who are not really doing anything. Have you ever seen an actor onstage who is supposed to be hungry and eating, but never eats the damn food? This is because they think the food will get in the way of how much they are wowing the audience with their clever ways of saying the words. This kind of acting makes me want to spit. If you are supposed to be hungry and eating some cereal, eat the cereal! Really do what you are doing! Have I made my point? I hope so. It is essential.

In short, we talked about the three factors that will lead to your acting being alive rather than dead:

1. You must listen with the ear of your heart.

2. You must live in the present moment.

3. You must really *do* the things you are doing onstage.

This is invigorating stuff and, when you tackle these acting skills, they will transform the quality of your acting in the most brilliant way.

CHAPTER FIVE

Truth 5 · The Fundamental Goal of Acting Technique

With so many different acting techniques, which should I choose? How do I know if it's a good one and if it will work for me? Which will teach me how to approach big emotions like crying and rage? These are the questions most acting students ask. In this chapter, we will get very clear on what makes a good acting technique. Then we'll answer the big question: Ultimately, what is the one, fundamental thing *all* acting techniques are really for?

First of all, if an acting technique is valid, it will help you arrive at the one, definitive truth—*your* truth. An acting technique is only legitimate if it helps you express completely who you truly are in each moment, rather than the person you think you should be or the person others tell you to be. This is exactly what Constantin Stanislavski, the great Russian actor, director, and acting teacher, was talking about when he said, "You are more interesting than the greatest actor who ever lived!" We don't need another Natalie Portman or Johnny Depp; we've already got those actors. What the audience is aching for is a wonderfully and authentically expressive you!

A good acting technique must also help you give up the need to control the other actors you are working with, your own responses, and what the audience thinks of you. This, of course, means you have to be willing to risk looking foolish, which most actors desperately avoid. The irony is, when you are totally yourself, you never look foolish! Once you have your attention completely off of yourself, your energy is freed up to be where it needs to be: on what is happening with your acting partners in the moment and on what you are doing.

Acting Is Action

As Sanford Meisner said, acting is doing. A healthy acting technique will instruct you that acting is not about what you think, feel, or say, acting is about what you actually *do*. Let me make this clear by expanding on an example I introduced in the last chapter: Imagine the person you love most in the world was trapped in a burning car. Where would all of your attention be?

In our discussion of the Reality of Doing in chapter 4, we established that your attention would be on getting the person out of the car. Now, in the midst of your attempt to get the person out of the car, would you stop to think, "I should break down and cry right now so everyone would see that I am truly upset" or "To break down and cry, I will take a minute to think about the time my puppy died five years ago"?

Of course you wouldn't have these thoughts! It is only bad actors that have these kinds of thoughts while they are acting. As you tried to rescue your loved one from the burning car, you would be so deeply involved in that action that your emotions would come to life in the most natural way. You might be terrified, shocked, enraged, and sad; you might scream, cry, or be totally silent. All of these emotions and all of your behavior would happen on their own as a by-product of your attempt to save your loved one's life. This is a big deal. Note that when you do something fully that has great meaning to you, your emotions come to life with no effort on your part!

When it comes to acting, the realm of the emotions is the most intangible and elusive. Working on your emotional instrument is vital, but it can also lead to very big traps for the acting student, so let's spend some time exploring it. To begin, we'll look at the history of modern acting and actors' training in our country.

Lee Strasberg and Affective Memory

In 1930, Stanislavski brought his Moscow Art Theater to New York City. Audiences were stunned to witness an acting company being realistic and human. Up until this time, acting was mostly fake and pretended. American plays were, for the most part, merely light entertainment.

Harold Clurman, Lee Strasberg, and Cheryl Crawford were inspired by the work of Stanislavski's troupe of actors. In 1931, they founded The Group Theatre. Over the course of the next ten years, out of their commitment to do plays that mirrored the troubled times of our country and to create a method of acting that was passionately alive and true, The Group Theatre would totally transform the quality of American theater.

During this period, Lee Strasberg created his interpretation of Stanislavski's acting technique; what we now call Method Acting. In Strasberg's Method, you would use the technique Strasberg called Affective Memory to be in an extremely emotional state. Here's how it works. Let's say you are playing the role of Vicki, and these are the first two lines of a scene:

FRANCES: My God, what happened? I have never seen you so upset!
VICKI: Oh, Frances, my mother died. What do I do? My mother died.

Obviously, because of the way Frances reacts when you make your entrance, Vicki must enter stage deeply shaken and utterly distraught. To fulfill this emotional demand using Affective Memory, you would find a parallel event from your past that had a similar emotional effect. This might be when your best friend died when you were young, leaving you heartbroken. Using another Method technique called Sense Memory, you go over in your mind all of the sensory aspects of the original event such as the details of the room you were in when you learned that your friend was dead, the clothes you were wearing, the objects that were all around you. You would try to see, hear, taste, feel, and smell all of the details of the original event.

Affective Memory is a very debilitating way of working. It is the cause of more emotional paralysis in actors than anything else I know. Let me tell you why, specifically, Affective Memory is at best unhealthy and, at worst, extremely dangerous.

Most importantly, the process of bringing up emotions from past events in our lives is not how we work as human beings. We do not sit around purposely trying to be emotional, and we do not try to re-live past events. Here's an example. Last February, I got a call from my sister that my mother was in the hospital. That same day, I flew down to Florida to see her. By the time I arrived, my mother was already dead and in a casket. I arrived too late. As you can imagine, all this was deeply disturbing and upsetting for me then, and it still is today. But I do not purposely sit around trying to re-live the whole event so I can be emotional. Human beings simply don't do that. As you know from the previous chapters, I am a firm believer that everything we do as an actor must relate to how we operate as human beings; otherwise, it is false.

Another incapacitating aspect of Affective Memory is that it does not relate to who you are and what has meaning to you in the present. It forces you to go back and try to be someone you were years before. Obviously, over time, your interpretation of the big events in your life changes. You are manipulating yourself to be someone you once were rather than the person you are today.

Affective Memory is also extremely limited. We all have only had a certain number of big events in our lives to draw from. So to fulfill the emotional demands of the many parts you will be playing, you would end up rehashing the same old events over and over and over. Not only is this a restrictive way of working but it is also an unhealthy way of working. You can imagine how reliving personal tragedies over and over again would drain you psychologically and tear your insides apart.

I have been told by friends who actually sat in on Strasberg's classes that his emphasis was not on Affective Memory, but it certainly has risen to prominence in the more recent Method classes. Often, Method training veers off into therapy rather than acting. Since the acting teacher is not a licensed therapist, this technique can be dangerous for your well-being.

To sum up, Affective Memory:

1. Is not related to how you operate as a human being.
2. Does not relate to who you are and what has meaning to you right now.
3. Is very limited.
4. Is an emotionally unhealthy and dangerous way of working.

Sanford Meisner and Emotional Preparation

So what can we do to bring our emotions safely and realistically to the stage? Let's reverse the shortcomings of Affective Memory to create the four essential requirements for a healthy, workable acting technique:

1. It relates to how you operate as a human being. In other words, it is an organic way of working.
2. It relates to who you are today and what has meaning to you right now.
3. It is totally unlimited.
4. It is an emotionally healthy and safe way of working.

As it turns out, there is a way of working with your own emotional instrument that meets these four essential requirements for a useful acting technique; one that matures in you as you grow in your life and in your art.

After the break up of The Group, Sanford Meisner, another member of the company, also went on to become a major acting teacher of our time. Meisner created his own approach to the training of actors, which differed from Strasberg's Method, particularly in the creation of emotion. Sanford Meisner uses a technique called Emotional Preparation that works with your imagination, rather than dredging up previous life events.

> Imagination is more important then knowledge. Knowledge is limited. Imagination encircles the world.
>
> ALBERT EINSTEIN

> Imagination is the eye of the soul.
>
> JOSEPH JOUBERT

What is Emotional Preparation? To make this very clear, let's go back to Vicki:

FRANCES: My God, what happened? I have never seen you so upset!
VICKI: Oh, Frances, my mother died. What do I do? My mother died.

In the Meisner Approach, you begin offstage with an "element of truth"—an important, real person from your life today. Then you picture this element of truth in dire, imaginative circumstances to reflect the what's happening in the scene. When you fully embrace the circumstances and make them intensely and intimately stimulating to you, they will result in a powerful emotional response. You make your entrance riding on this wave of emotion!

So does Emotional Preparation fulfill our four essential requirements for a healthy, workable acting technique?

1. Emotional Preparation is a truly organic way of working because, as human beings, all of us have vivid imaginations and a rich fantasy life. The only difference between this acting work and real life is that in life we usually only permit our fantasies to go so far, whereas in our acting we must permit our fantasy to go into the most extreme places.
2. Since you are creating the fantasy in the moment based on something that has significance in your life today, the Emotional Preparation is related to who you are right now rather than who you were in the past.
3. When you use your imagination to create your circumstances, the possibilities are as unlimited and infinite as your imagination.
4. Emotional Preparation is a healthy way of working because the circumstances are *imaginary.*

Let's go back to Vicki to flesh out this final point. Maybe you prepare for your entrance by imagining that your own mother was walking down the street and was hit from behind by a speeding motorcycle. She is in critical condition; the doctors say that she has very little chance to survive. Just the thought of this terrible event makes you feel sick inside and deeply disturbed. Now it makes complete sense for the actress playing the part of Frances to say as you enter, "My God, what happened? I have never seen you so upset!" While this technique is effective, it is not unhealthy because when the play is over, you can call your mother on the phone and reassure yourself that she is fine.

Not only is Emotional Preparation a healthier way of working, it is also much more persuasive because people are far more willing to take on disturbing and extreme events when they are invented rather than when they are dredged-up from the past. Do you see how much human sense all this makes? (If you want to learn more about how to work with Emotional Preparation, my book *The Sanford Meisner Approach: Workbook Two, Emotional Freedom* will train you step-by-step.)

The Ultimate Goal

Let's face it, acting is an emotional art form. All plays and screenplays are based on characters living in the midst of the most extreme events. This places huge emotional demands on actors, and it is part of the great thrill of acting. At the same time, emotion must never be the aim of your acting; it is always the by-product of what you are *doing*, as we discussed at the beginning of this chapter. So no matter how emotional you become, it is all a waste of energy if you are not learning how to actually "do" onstage. A good acting technique will train you to fight for your life and to strive to accomplish your goals with every ounce of your being.

Let's get back to the question from the beginning of the chapter: "Ultimately, what is the one, fundamental thing all valuable acting techniques are really for?"

Here's my answer: to help you become willing, able, and strong enough to allow the miracle of creation to occur.

Great acting is, indeed, an act of creation. We are talking about moving our ego out of the way and allowing something much more powerful to speak through us. We are talking about lifting the words off a piece of paper and infusing them with life. We are talking about taking a journey, which involves huge risks! We are talking about passion, urgency, high stakes, and action against all odds! These, my friend, are no small things! And they lead to the most vibrant, thrilling life I know.

As I mentioned earlier, Sanford Meisner was my teacher. The work I did in his classes truly transformed my life. Am I biased when it comes to acting technique? Of course I am. But this bias is the result of twenty-five years of experience as an actor, director, author, and teacher of acting. Literally, my whole adult life has been devoted to the Meisner approach. I have a strong conviction that it is the best, most organic, and healthiest technique of acting available; nothing else comes close. I offer this technique to you because I believe it, and I know it works. If you commit to it, you will be rewarded.

CHAPTER SIX

Truth 6 • Acting Is an Act of Commitment

Life truly lived is a risky business, and, if one puts up too many fences against risk, one ends by shutting out life itself.

KENNETH S. DAVIS

Many people talk about commitment very casually, but when difficulties arise, they drop their commitment as easy as spitting out a piece of gum because the sweetness is gone. It is important to understand that true commitment to anything involves great difficulties and tests one's ability to endure. There is a Chinese proverb that says that, "The gem cannot be polished without friction, nor man perfected without trials." E. M. Gray said it this way:

> The successful person has the habit of doing things failures don't like to do. They don't like doing them either necessarily. But their disliking is subordinated to the strength of their purpose.

The Deeper Wish

The signposts of commitment are the things we choose to do and the choices we make every day. Commitment is hard to see and identify because it springs from what I like to call a "deeper wish." What is a deeper wish? Our deeper wish is what gets us out of bed every morning and propels us to take action. Now the actions we take may be simple or they may be monumental. Regardless, these daily actions allow us to measure out commitment. It is always more accurate to examine our commitment by looking at the things we actually do than by what we say.

Why is it so important to understand and get in touch with our own deeper wish? By becoming conscious of our deeper wish, we get a very clear sense of direction in our life. As an actor, it is exactly what we will have to do every time we attempt to bring a character to life because every character in every well-written play also has his or her roots firmly grounded in a specific deeper wish.

Other acting terms used for the deeper wish of a character are *spine, major objective, super objective,* or *arc.* The deeper wish is simply the primary thing the character is trying to accomplish before the play begins and continues to try to accomplish after the play ends.

Let's take a look at the last sentence once more. I didn't say that the character is trying to accomplish something from the moment the play begins; I said that the character is trying to accomplish something from *before* the play begins. And I didn't say he or she is finished with the deeper wish when the play ends, I said that he or she continues to try to accomplish these things *after* the play ends. Think of it this way, did you just appear and come to life when you picked up this book? And do you suddenly disappear when you put the book down? Of course not! You came to reading this book with a whole life filled with hopes and longings and things you did and didn't do and dreamed of doing, *then* you started to read this book. When you put the book down, you will continue to have a whole life filled with hopes and longings, things you will do and not do and things you will dream of doing. The character in a play is no different; he or she does not suddenly appear on page one and suddenly disappear on page 106. When you connect with a character's deeper wish, the audience will see the character as a fully living and breathing human being.

To find the deeper wish, examine the script and discover all of the things the character does, all the things he or she hopes to do, all the things he or she chooses not to do, and all the things he or she dreams of doing. I love the phrase "the deeper wish" because it implies that the desire is absolutely personal and, because it is so intense, it becomes intrinsically active and leads to the taking of action.

The best way to begin a discussion about the deeper wish is not with interesting answers but with great questions:

> What am I willing to risk everything for?
> What is necessary to me?
> What is as important to me as the air I breathe?
> What am I truly devoted to?

Again, because you will have to get onto intimate terms with the deeper wish of every character you will play, it is useful to first get onto intimate terms with your own deeper wish. At the top of a page in your journal, I want you to write the phrase, "My Deeper Wish." Then, I want you to close your eyes and think about what you are after in this life, what is driving you. Then begin to write your discoveries in your journal. Examine all of the things you have done in the past, all of the things you are doing with your life right now, and all of the things you dream about doing. Each time you write down something, ask yourself why each item is important and see what you are lead to next. Here is an example of what a deeper wish writing exercise might look like:

My Deeper Wish

I really want to act. I love acting and I think about it all the time. I love to be in the plays and go to rehearsals. I love reading the play over and over and thinking about the character's life. I love my acting class and I want to take more acting classes to get better and better. I love going to plays and movies and watching actors and wondering how they worked on their parts. I don't like missing my acting classes and I wish I had more time to devote to my acting. I really want to act and be an actor.

(Ask yourself, "Why?")

So I can be successful. So I can be a successful actor and work.

("Why?")

So I can be in stage productions as well as in big movies.

("Why?")

So I can act out beautiful stories written by wonderful writers.

("Why?")

So that I can reach people, reach a lot of people all around the world.

("Why?")

So that I can make a difference in their lives.

("Why?")

So that people will stop hurting each other. Yes, I want people to stop hurting each other.

Do you see how the process works? Keep up the writing and keep asking yourself why until you feel like you have reached the bottom line of your own deeper wish. This can take a few moments to complete or it might take years. Either way, it is a very useful process to tackle in understanding what is vitally important to you and what you are truly committed to.

Now do the same exercise as a character from a play you might be working on right now. First write down all of the things the character has done, what he or she is doing now, and what he or she hopes to do. This will help you see the one, major objective of this character. It is this through-line that all of the character's actions spring from.

Acting Against All Odds

If you hear a voice within you say, "You cannot paint," then by all means paint and that voice will be silenced.

VINCENT VAN GOGH

Just as you are on a quest to fulfill your deeper wish against the odds, so is every character in every script. One recent film is a great example of this: *Cinderella Man*, the story of James J. Braddock, a Depression-era boxer. Braddock is on his way to becoming a championship boxer when a combination of a badly broken right hand and the stock market crash of 1929, where all of his earnings were invested, sends him into a downward spiral.

Unable to take care of his wife and three small children, Braddock goes to work on the docks and takes money from public assistance. He is soon offered one more chance to box. Motivated by the need to care for his family, he accepts the challenge even though all outside forces are against him—including a bout with a heavyweight champ who previously killed two men in the ring. Ultimately, it is the combination of his own inner drive and a strong left hand developed by his work on the docks, which lead to his redemption and victory. Braddock becomes the heavyweight championship of the world.

Another film that shows people acting against all odds is the documentary *Born Into Brothels*. Photographer/photojournalist Zana Briski originally went to Calcutta to capture on film the lives of the prostitutes in the red light district. However, it was the children of these women who captured Briski's heart and ultimately became the subject of this film. Against all odds—

poverty, injustice, bureaucracy, etc.—the filmmaker finds she must fight for these children's welfare. Zana Briski's courage and devotion to follow her inner voice without worrying about results is profoundly moving. Of course, the children also persevere against great odds. Their courage, wisdom, and vitality, even in the most oppressive environment, are also an inspiration.

So what is the prize for risking everything, for committing our entire being to what we know is essential, even though the odds may be against us? The prize is aliveness! Life is not casual. The stakes are always high. Every moment is filled with earth-shaking potential. It is only in sleepwalking through our lives that we forget the stakes involved. We get lulled into the false idea that we can control our environment and that tomorrow will be just as we expect it to be. The truth is that life is completely unpredictable, unexpected, surprising, and greater than we think it is. Ultimately, it is in understanding our own commitment that, like buoys on the water, can help keep us in the channel of life and off of the rocks.

But if we find our deeper wish and commitment, can we still "hit the rocks"? All of us make mistakes sometimes—big mistakes. I call this being "out of alignment with our lives." Just like when our spines are out of alignment, there is pain involved. Big mistakes have consequences that have to be dealt with, and there is a struggle to get our lives back in the right direction. I am telling you all of this because it is the same with the character in the play; he or she also makes big mistakes and takes actions that are not in alignment with his or her own spine (or deeper wish). But in knowing what the character's deeper wish really is, you will have a clear sense of the ramifications involved, and how hard you will have to struggle to get back on track.

Most of the important things in the world have been accomplished by people who have kept on trying when there seemed to be no hope at all.

DALE CARNEGIE

The major message of this chapter is that acting, when you boil it down to its core, is an act of commitment. It is true for both the character in the script and for you, the artist. Most people who approach the acting profession eventually drop by the wayside; they are not up for the tremendous rigors involved and are not clear on their own commitment. But when you are intimately in touch with your own deeper wish and when you have become clear why you are involved in this most beautiful art form, you have at your disposal a true furnace of power that will sustain you both when life is smooth and when times get rough.

CHAPTER SEVEN

Truth 7 • Auditioning Is Not What You Think

Fun is fundamental. There is no way around it. You absolutely must have fun. Without fun, there is no enthusiasm. Without enthusiasm, there is no energy. Without energy, there are only shades of gray.

DOUG HALL

Very few actors truly enjoy auditioning, which is unfortunate because auditioning goes hand in hand with the profession of acting. To be effective in your auditions, you have to find a way to get pleasure from them; if you are not having fun, neither will the people watching you. Of course, a certain amount of anxiety over auditioning is natural. Being nervous is a sign that what you are doing matters to you. If it didn't mean a thing in the world to you, you wouldn't be nervous.

Pleasing "Them"

A good audition is a great performance. Often when actors begin auditioning, they focus more on getting the job then on performing well. When you become results-oriented, you strive to give "them" (the director, producer, casting director, or agent) what you imagine they want. If you put the emphasis of the audition on pleasing, you take away your power and put it into the hands of the director, casting director, or agent. This creates a wave of fear that paralyzes your creative center and sabotages your capacity to perform well.

As we established earlier, we do not have control over what other people do or how other people think or feel about us. This is also important to remember when it comes to auditioning. Just as you cannot make someone fall in love with you, you also cannot make the director give you a job. The only thing you have control over in this life is what *you* do. This basic truth will empower your auditions. You should not and cannot make "them" like you. When you accept this, you can go in to do your job in the most alive and passionate way you know how. And this is exactly what every good director wants to see. He or she wants you to come in to the audition as a strong, creative artist giving an alive and passionate performance.

The truth is, "they" do not really know what they want. Casting a play or a movie is a very tough job. The casting decisions are critical. What you have to understand is that the director wants to like you. The director doesn't want to see a phony you trying to be something you're not; he is hoping you will come in and be completely yourself, as you inhabit the role that you are auditioning for. He may have some ideas about what type or quality he is looking for, but good casting requires an open mind. I have heard many stories of directors who changed their minds after seeing a great audition.

Auditioning + You = Fun

You must go into the audition to please yourself first and your own artistic standards. Follow through on your own vision of what the part in the script is about and live it out fully in every moment! When you do this, the director will know she has witnessed something extraordinary. You may get the part or you may not. If you do not get this part (for reasons out of your control), you and your performance will be remembered. The director may call you back three years later for another role. It happens all the time.

When you truly put the emphasis on doing a great performance rather than on getting the job, you have taken the power back into your own hands and you can begin to actually enjoy your auditions. With this attitude, you discover a deep state of relaxation, which frees up your creative juices, your inner strength, and your passion to perform. Auditioning can really become fun! Remember that no matter what the part is and no matter what the emotional demands are, ultimately acting must be fun or why would anyone face the continual rigors of doing it?

What Casting Directors Want

The casting director's job is to get the best actors in to audition and to help make casting decisions. Recently, I had a conversation with New York City casting director Stephanie Klapper of Stephanie Klapper Casting. Let's hear directly from a great casting director and get her take on auditioning:

The most difficult thing for an actor to do is to be themselves when they walk in the room. A lot of the audition, in addition to the work you are going to do, is about the contact you make with the people casting the production. What I look for is a sense of your personality in addition to your acting capability. You have such a short amount of time—it's from five to seven minutes, if that—in which you have to establish an instant relationship and do your piece and feel successful about it. To me, it's about eye contact, it's about how you greet the person, and it's about how you introduce yourself and your material. Of course, we factor in that there are going to be nerves, but how do you manage that and get beyond it?

The trap in auditions is doing what you think we want you to do and, therefore, second-guessing yourself. Especially if you are younger, you have to trust who you are as a person at this point. You must have your life and vibrancy—you don't have to get rid of that—and still you must be appropriate for the audition (and by appropriate I mean polite and well put together).

No matter what stage you are at as actors, I do listen to your speech and how you talk, it's really important to me that you speak well. If it's a comedy, I love to laugh. And I love to see what your connection to the material is, just as with the dramatic piece. I also love for the audition piece to be something that is appropriate for you as a young actor.

What is exciting to me is to see you, the human being, inside your audition material. It's a trap if you are over-directed to be the character and not bring yourself to it; that shortchanges both you and the material. We don't get a good sense of who you are as an actor because we just see what you have been told to do. Especially for young actors, it's the spirit of the person we are looking for.

Nerves have a way of deadening one's hearing ability. If you have a director who wants to see if you are versatile and wants to see if you are flexible, you need to be aware of that and be able to follow directions— and that it is not meant as a criticism. It's like when you go to the gym and you work out, you may have poor form and you may hurt yourself and someone may correct you for your benefit. But also, the director may want to see if you can make adjustments that are in line with his or her vision of what the material is. So it is very important that you are flexible. This goes back to not being over-directed because then you get stuck. Many directors want to make sure that you are not stuck and that you have a wide range and a big palette of colors available to work with.

Passion and aliveness are the most valuable qualities you could ask for in an actor; it is the drive that is going to help you in the long run if you are going to stay with it. You need to have passion because you are going to go through a lot of times that are not so easy. It's a profession and a job that is always testing us, on both sides of the table, and the more passion and drive you have, the more longevity you have. You need that and a strong sense of person.

It is also very tempting for young actors, because of their love of acting and passion for acting, not to get a well-rounded education. You may think that you don't need to be well educated outside of your acting, and I think this is a tremendous mistake. So much of your work and your creativity come from other places inside yourself. It is important that you take classes in other things besides acting because you must constantly grow and evolve as a person. I have to tell you that an actor who is stupid does not do me any good.

I love when an actor comes in and, because of his or her performance in the audition, changes the mindset of where the director thought he wanted to go with the part. But it depends on the openness of the director. The best director is the one who is open to all possibilities. But just like actors, some directors get stuck and aren't open enough to change what their concept is because it may be safe for them. Of course you hope you will have a director who will work with you because you want a good match, an actor and director who can be inventive together.

Last advice? Research what you are auditioning for. Learn a little about whom you are auditioning for ahead of time. If you are doing a musical audition, be prepared to work with either a good accompanist or a bad accompanist. You may get an accompanist that is not very good and that can undermine your audition, so you must know your music super well. For plays, get a hold of the script ahead of time. If you are doing a monologue, make sure it is a monologue that's fitting to the type of material you are auditioning for. Dress appropriately. It's a job interview; dress in a way that's comfortable to move around in but that also shows you off well. Be organized. Have pictures and résumés that are the right size and that are stapled properly to each other, and have extra copies—saying you forgot it is not an excuse. You can't make excuses. No matter where you are coming from, you have to present yourself in a professional manner because we are seeing you on a level playing field with everyone else. In the hallway before the audition, make sure that you are not sucked into the social life that is going on out there but that you have your time. You have your moment to be away to prepare yourself to do what you need to do.

What is the most important message you can take away from Stephanie's words? It is that from the time you enter the audition room until the time you leave, it is you, the human being, who must shine through. The people casting the production are not looking for some highly directed concept in your performance (thus the title of this chapter, "Auditioning Is Not What You *Think*"). Rather, they want to see a living, breathing human being acting with tremendous passion and aliveness, an actor who is flexible and willing to make adjustments based on the needs of the director.

And hasn't that been the major through-line of this whole book? Everything we do as actors must spring from our humanity, which is what makes us truly unique and one-of-a-kind. We have established in many ways and from every angle that acting is a living, creative process and it demands that we be really awake in every moment. Acting is a craft. We must face the rigors head on and strive toward mastery no matter the difficulties. In taking risks and fighting for what is most important to us, we are brought to life.

The audience wants to fall in love with you. They have purchased their tickets and made time in their lives to see you perform. They want to love you. If you give them a simple, honest, and passionate performance, you will remind them that they, too, are human beings. When you work authentically, you touch the audience in a very deep way. You are a gift in their lives. This is when you, the artist, make a true difference. Though the real work may be difficult, isn't that worth striving for? I say it is; it is worth every moment of the struggle! In striving for connection, struggle soon turns into pure joy.

> Everyone should carefully observe which way
> his heart draws him, and then choose that way
> with all his strength.
>
> ANONYMOUS

I hope you have enjoyed my book. I hope it will be useful to you as you chart your own course in your life and in your art. I wish you a most wonderful journey filled with extraordinary and exciting experiences and great health to support all of your endeavors.

Quotes to Live By

Talk doesn't cook rice.

CHINESE PROVERB

Care about people's approval, and you will be their prisoner.

CHINESE PROVERB

If you let yourself be blown to and fro, you lose touch with your roots.

CHINESE PROVERB

The journey of a thousand miles begins with a single step.

LAO-TSE

Your vision will become clear only when you can look into your own heart.

CARL JUNG

The past has flown away. The coming month and year do not exist. Ours only is the present's tiny point.

MAHMUD SHABISTARI

If a man carries his own lantern, he need not fear darkness.

HASIDIC SAYING

Worry never robs tomorrow of its sorrow; it only saps today of its strength.

A.J. CRONIN

If we do not change our direction, we are likely to end up where we are headed.

ANCIENT CHINESE PROVERB

To improve the golden moment of opportunity, and catch the good that is within our reach, is the great art of life.

SAMUEL JOHNSON

The ability to simplify means to eliminate the unnecessary so that the necessary may speak.

HANS HOFMANN

It is the chiefest point of happiness that a man is willing to be what he is.

DESIDERIUS ERASMUS

We are what we repeatedly do. Excellence, then, is not an act, but a habit.

ARISTOTLE

If one advances confidently in the direction of his dreams, and endeavors to live the life which he has imagined, he will meet with success unexpected in common hours.

HENRY DAVID THOREAU

If you understand, things are just as they are; if you do not understand, things are just as they are.

ZEN PROVERB

The intellect has little to do on the road to discovery. There comes a leap in consciousness, call it intuition or what you will, and the solution comes to you and you don't know how or why.

ALBERT EINSTEIN

All the beautiful sentiments in the world weigh less than a single lovely action.

JAMES RUSSELL LOWELL

Real generosity toward the future consists in giving all to what is present.

ALBERT CAMUS

If you work on your mind with your mind, how can you avoid an immense confusion?

SENG-TS'AN

It does not matter how slowly you go, so long as you do not stop.

CONFUCIUS

If you have built castles in the air, your work need not be lost; that is where they should be. Now put foundations under them.

HENRY DAVID THOREAU

Great Spirit, help me never to judge another until I have walked in his moccasins.

SIOUX INDIAN PRAYER

The harder we try to catch hold of the moment, to seize a pleasant sensation, the more elusive it becomes. It is like trying to clutch water in one's hands—the harder one grips, the faster it slips through one's fingers.

ALAN WATTS

Remind me each day that the race is not always to the swift; that there is more to life than increasing its speed. Let me look upward into the towering oak and know that it grew great and strong because it grew slowly and well.

ORIN L. CRAIN

Your proper concern is alone the action of duty, not the fruits of the action. Cast then away all desire and fear for the fruits, and perform your duty.

BHAGAVAD GITA

Life can only be understood backwards, but it must be lived forwards.

SOREN KIERKEGAARD

Even if I knew that tomorrow the world would go to pieces, I would still plant my apple tree.

MARTIN LUTHER

Art is a collaboration between God and the artist, and the less the artist does the better.

ANDRE GIDE

I saw the angel in the marble and carved until I set him free.

MICHELANGELO

Art attracts us only by what it reveals of our most secret self.

JEAN-LUC GODARD

If you ask me what I came to do in this world, I, an artist, I will answer you: 'I came to live out loud.'

EMILE ZOLA

Growth demands a temporary surrender of security.

GAIL SHEEHY

All growth is a leap in the dark, a spontaneous unpremeditated act without the benefit of experience.

HENRY MILLER

Life is either a daring adventure or nothing. To keep our faces toward change and behave like free spirits in the presence of fate is strength undefeatable.

HELEN KELLER

Make the most of yourself, for that is all there is of you.

RALPH WALDO EMERSON

We should take care not to make the intellect our god; it has, of course, powerful muscles, but no personality.

ALBERT EINSTEIN

A good heart is better than all the heads in the world.

EDWARD BULWER-LYTTON

What lies behind us and what lies before us are tiny matters compared to what lies within us.

OLIVER WENDELL HOLMES

Critics are like eunuchs in a harem: they know how it's done, they've seen it done every day, but they're unable to do it themselves.

BRENDAN BEHAN

A bad review is even less important than whether it is raining in Patagonia.

IRIS MURDOCH

The public is the only critic whose opinion is worth anything at all.

MARK TWAIN

Pay no attention to what the critics say; no statue has ever been erected to a critic.

JEAN SIBELIUS

The expectations of life depend upon diligence; the mechanic that would perfect his work must first sharpen his tools.

CONFUCIUS

Amateurs hope. Professionals work.

GARSON KANIN

It is no use saying, 'We are doing our best.' You have got to succeed in doing what is necessary.

WINSTON CHURCHILL

The only place where success comes before work is in a dictionary.

VIDAL SASSOON

The winds and waves are always on the side of the ablest navigators.

EDWARD GIBBON

I long to accomplish a great and noble task, but it is my chief duty to accomplish small tasks as if they were great and noble.

HELEN KELLER

Nothing is more simple than greatness; indeed, to be simple is to be great.

RALPH WALDO EMERSON

Many persons have a wrong idea of what constitutes true happiness. It is not attained through self-gratification but through fidelity to a worthy purpose.

HELEN KELLER

Winning is important, but what brings me real joy is the experience of being fully engaged in whatever I'm doing.

PHIL JACKSON

Cherish your visions and your dreams as they are the children of your soul; the blue prints of your ultimate achievements.

NAPOLEON HILL

You see things; and you say 'Why?' But I dream things that never were; and I say 'Why not'?

> GEORGE BERNARD SHAW

Some of the world's greatest feats were accomplished by people not smart enough to know they were impossible.

> DOUG LARSON

Real love is a pilgrimage. It happens when there is no strategy, but it is very rare because most people are strategists.

> ANITA BROOKNER

Darkness cannot drive out darkness; only light can do that. Hate cannot drive out hate; only love can do that.

> MARTIN LUTHER KING JR.

No love, no friendship can cross the path of our destiny without leaving some mark on it forever.

> FRANCOIS MAURIAC

Be glad of life, because it gives you the chance to love and to work and to play and to look up at the stars.

> HENRY VAN DYKE

Still around the corner there may wait
A new road, or a secret gate.

> J.R.R. TOLKIEN

There is not enough darkness in the world to put out the light of even one small candle.

> ROBERT ALDEN

There is a Zen story about a man who studied with a master for a while, and told the master, "I want the truth." And the master said, "Cut trees for a while." So the student cut trees for about six or eight months. Finally, he reminded the master, "I've been asking you for the truth." The master replied, "Go out and turn all those trees into charcoal." So the student did that for about six months, and the master never spoke to him. Finally, the young man said, "Listen, master, I'm leaving you. I told you I wanted the truth." The master said, "Let me walk with you a way." They walked together until they came over a bridge. Under it, there was rushing water. The master gave the student a shove, sending him into the water. He slipped under the surface. "I can't swim!" he cried. Down again, "I can't swim!" The third time, the master pulled him up onto bridge, and said, "Now, when you want truth the same way you wanted that breath of air, you've already got it."

Larry Silverberg is considered the foremost authority on the Sanford Meisner technique of acting through his internationally acclaimed four-volume series, *The Sanford Meisner Approach: An Actors Workbook,* and his book *Loving To Audition.*

Larry is a graduate of the Neighborhood Playhouse School of Theatre where he studied with legendary acting teacher, Sanford Meisner. Since then, Larry has worked professionally as an actor and director across the United States and in Canada. Most recently, he received high praise from the *New York Times* for his performance as Don in Athol Fugard's *People Are Living There* at The Signature Theater in New York City, and he won the Seattle Critic's Association "Stellar Acting Award" for his portrayal of Teach in the Belltown Theatre Center production of *American Buffalo.*

Larry teaches acting in his world-renowned professional actors training program, "The Meisner Intensive Training Program," which he runs in New York City. Larry also teaches visiting master classes at universities, colleges and acting studios around the globe. Larry can be contacted through his web site address at www.actorscraft.com.

Loving to Audition

The Audition Workbook for Actors
by Larry Silverberg

"A valuable, adventurous, and enthusiastic entrée into the little defined world of auditioning."

Allan Miller, actor, director, teacher, and author

"Acting coach Larry Silverberg takes two monologues and proceeds for 147 pages to dissect every word, every possible layer of meaning, every possible angle of approach, to show how a master actor would interpret the speeches at an audition. Silverberg supplies so many techniques for climbing inside the brief texts that any actor with the presence of mind to recall a tenth of them in the heat of a real-life audition would have the basis for ample calm confidence. This is a really useful guide for absorbing text quickly — whether for performer or audience."

Drama, Dance, and Theater Editor's
Recommended Book, Amazon.com

includes specific exercises
LOVING TO AUDITION
ISBN 1-57525-007-1, 144 pages, $15.95

Published by Smith and Kraus, Inc.
Available at your local bookstore
or call toll-free (888) 282-2881 www.SmithandKraus.com